ARCHWAY's

GARDEN

RHYMES

Archie E. Anderson

ARCHWAY'S GARDEN SEASON

A Mythbreaker Book

First Edition

© Copyright 2013 Archie Edgar Anderson (1917-) & Donald Murray Anderson (1950-)
All photographs in this book © Copyright 2013 Archie Edgar Anderson (1917-) & Donald Murray Anderson (1950-)

All rights reserved. Without limiting rights under copyright reserved above, no part of this book may be reproduced, stored in or introduced into a retrieval system, or transmitted in any form or by any means (electronic, mechanical, photocopying, recording, or otherwise) without prior written permission of the copyright owner.

For information address: mythsbreaker@myway.com

Archie is an amateur gardener. He does it all for love and gains great pleasure from the work and its pleasing effects on others. His gardening is a work of love, a feeling he expresses both in the earth, in a few photographs, and in many poems.

Archie's gardening begins in one of the cruelest climates for plant life in the northern hemisphere, northern Alberta, where the growing season can be cut short by frost and snow before the end of the often very short, late summer.

Fortunately, most of the next 60 years of his gardening work, so far, is much less of a struggle. Archie continues his planting, watering, weeding, pruning, and caring in in a far more moderate and hospitable climate for growing, on the Pacific Coast of Canada.

Year-in-the-life

Plant-ation

Others' Rows

Year-in-the-life

Con-Seeded?

With great hope, first garden planted,

Just about three score years ago.

All seed catalogues, soon found out,

Exaggerate how plants do grow.

Garden skills grew over the years:

Late or early, each prairie frost

Was constant challenge to be met.

Sometimes won, but more often lost.

With some seed, experimented;

Produced potato, rhubarb too.

With such great promise seemed to hold.

To expand yield, knew what to do.

Took weekend off: returned to find

Potatoes frozen in the ground.

Hopes were dashed by a killing frost:

Pulled up stakes; soon for West Coast bound.

Milder climate brought great delight,

As gardening was simple act,

Did little more than plant some seeds,

And then from growing plants quickly backed.

Technique, of course, far from perfect.

Admit to making odd blunder.

For recent one, have no excuse:

It must indeed make one wonder.

Do start sweet peas from seed each year,

But was away at proper time,

Which meant, for blossoms to ensure,

Buying plants which would reach their prime.

Seedlings did well and grew apace.

Soon many flowers came in sight.

To great surprise, no coloured ones;

Every single blossom was white.

Too soon, pea pods began to form;

Embarrassing, to say the least.

Though can't tell sweet from from garden type,

The benefit was truly feast.

Ex-Seeded?

Banana plant did lead the way.

Ancestor plantain had black seed,

And was quite starchy to the taste.

Seedless banana now in lead.

Though most grapes have now followed suit,

Still are left a few ones seeded.

No stoned fruit have made seedless leap

So, much more research is needed.

Special case is watermelon.

Some are seed free, is sellers' boast.

If you discount small white pips,

Indeed are seedless -- well, almost.

There is one fruit, may never change,

Will remain as firm as granite.

And, of course, you've already guessed,

No other than pomegranate.

Garden For Life

Each person's life is garden,

Which they shape by thoughts and deeds.

Some seem to grow and prosper,

While others fail, chocked by weeds.

Some hid behind wall or fence,

While some open up and share.

Some let blossoms fade away,

And really don't seem to care.

Some, in autumn of their lives,

Find everything bare and bleak,

Others, have a harvest rich

With happiness all should seek.

It can never be too late,

Your life-garden to renew.

Don't wait for harsh winter blast –

Cultivate a bloom or two.

Eliminate all your weeds;

Pessimism, and defeat.

You'll soon find, at any age,

Your life can be full and sweet.

Green Out

What's this about green thumb,

The one that makes all things grow,

From vegetables to flowers

That always lead garden show?

Have enjoyed the growing game;

Take delight in planting seeds.

Some success, and failures too;

Often more than share of weeds.

Have checked thumbs for sign of green,

But that colour always lack,

As often come from garden;

Thumbs aren't green – - but often black.

Once thought my thumbs could be green,

So made a close inspection,

Only to discover that

Was only lawn reflection

Spring parade

Flamboyant flags of spring

Wave away the winter's cold;

Fresh season painted with

Mauve and white and flaming gold.

As colour party leads,

Early morning winter nip

Fights rear-guard action as

It chills wine of spring we sip.

Cold dark days of winter

Flee before spotlight of spring,

With shades of gold and mauve

Glowing as the robins sing.

Awakening

Pale snow drops timid, winter wan,

Poke through dead leaves to peak around;

Though spent from struggle, do remind

Life springs anew from barren ground.

Blithe, gay-frocked crocus soon leap forth

With purple, orange, on slender stems;

Full colour carpet laid for spring—

Tall daffodils with crocus hems.

The bursting buds, bulbs boisterous bloom

Of hyacinths and tulips too.

Almost unseen, mauve midget eyes

Of grey green daphne primly view.

Forsythia gives magic touch,

Waves golden wand to light the world;

Countless blooms, flags and pennants fly,

Their spring pastels and tints unfurled.

As flaming blossoms reach the trees,

Spring colours mount ever higher

Till rosy froth blots out the sky

And cherry trees glow pinkest fire.

The drowsy earth stirs fitfully;

As robin starts his noisy shout,

Spring's warm, moist hand, gives final shove;

Retreat of winter is a rout.

Spring Bonus

Gold and scarlet pennants wave

In spring parade's vanguard;

Brown and somber cherry tree

Stands naked in the yard.

Then, gaunt branch fingers stretch,

Bud caps are tossed to ground;

Blush pink blossoms quickly

Spread every branch around.

Wondrous glory is so brief;

Rose blooming masquerade

Dominates the garden scene

As pink cloud leads parade.

Old tree sighs as blooms desert,

Wind combs out tattered shreds;

Pink snow drifts to cover lawn,

Bulb blooms return to beds.

Ornamental cherry brings

No fruit for cherry bowl;

Far more precious gift bestows;

Sweet food for human soul.

Pink Promise

What of proud, pink, ruffled

Mistress of the Spring

Who flaunted blooms for all

To behold and sing?

The juice of heaven poured

Pitiless on pride,

Pounding beauty clusters

To a pink lawn tide.

Drooping and bedraggled,

Hang limp limbs in shame;

Few rags of tattered blooms

Faded beauty claims.

Memory of past glory

Fingers few pale shreds;

From pink to summer green,

Flimsy finery sheds.

As dignity returns,

Monarch shrugs off rain,

For there'll be other years;

Beauty blooms again.

Spring And Summer Views

Saw pale legged poplars poke
Their green plumes so fresh among
The winter weary, darkly
Drab, spruce and fir once so young.

Ever frantic flags of spring
Freshly robe the mountain slope,
Whispering their chorus of
A new season, and new hope.

They cling close to giants' base,
Seek not to climb craggy height:
They dip their roots in clear, cool
Streams that chatter with delight.

Nature's towers tolerate
Tiny scratches humans make
To set forth their feeble claims,
Amid rock, and tree, and lake.

Where ages are as minutes,
Human works may wear away,
But hills they call mountains
May for now and ever stay.

Sage brush clad in dusty green,
Squats on sere and sandy slope,
While the grooves on distant hills
Show where nature once did grope.

Barren heaps so dusty dry,

Slide to valleys lush, below,
Where rivers rush, lakes give pause,
Time drifts on as tall trees grow.

Met full force of prairie storm
Day, by cloud-burst, drowned in night.
Fiery sword the heavens split
And rumbling clouds shook with fright.

Storm pushed back by bluest blue,
With new dawn seemed that never
Elements had roared in wrath
As if the earth to sever.

Green and gold of countryside,
Cut by road, man's endeavour,
Promised land, where one can see,
One mile beyond forever.

Prostrate bands of gold await
Gaunt sentinels set to hoard
Awhile, treasure of the plains
Nature on our land has poured.

Now we gather to enjoy
Harvest of our summer days,
Sharing holidays recalled
As we took our several ways.

But Softly

It can be said much better,

(Or so the florists say)

When it is said with flowers;

But do they show the way?

Who will speak for violet?

It's surely far too shy

Daisy will, of course, not tell;

It will not even try.

Rose position is not clear;

It may use pseudonym;

Petunia could trumpet out

If it weren't quite so prim.

Snap-dragon may have the mouth

But seems to lack the voice.

Saying it with flowers seems

To be a hopeless choice.

If the dandelion could roar,

And asters weren't so mum,

Flowers could be on the scent;

And even bees would hum.

With flowers you may say it,

But when the petals fall

May their beauty and perfume

Oft waft in sweet recall.

Growing On

Have a private mini-jungle,

Without a sign of fearsome beast.

Some slugs and earwigs are around;

Such beastly things that nightly feast.

There also is a fence patrol

Of squirrels by day, racoons by night;

From time to time a pesky cat

To send birds in a panic flight.

Despite the hazards, some plants grow;

New flowers bloom when old ones fade.

Though at times it may seem messy,

There always is a bloom parade.

Kiwis provide some greenhouse shade,

To moderate the summer's heat,

And, in the Fall, they do provide

The most delicious fruit to eat.

Persimmon, plum, rose and lily

Compete in somewhat crowded place.

So far, it seems, the roses are

Barely ahead in growing race.

There's always room for one more plant

Around the garden jungle plot.

Not to worry, as always is

A corner for a plant in pot.

Front garden fashioned by the birds.

(Or, should the wind get credit too?)

Three mountain ash, birch and cherry,

Once started, grew, and grew and grew.

As for the harvest, it's a breeze;

Strawberry pots have first call;

Raspberry picking is next, then

Kiwi, grapes, before frost does fall.

There follows next, brief winter rest.

Perhaps some snow, but always rain.

In January things pick up

As bulbs begin to bloom again.

Jungle Jumble?

It's a jungle, called a garden:

For one more plant there's always room.

Each and every seed that's planted

Brings no promise sure of bloom.

They are a rather touchy lot;

They stab and scratch quite a bit.

No need to take my word for this;

My scratches are proof of it.

There is a plant that does attack;

To tear my skin and my clothes.

Would you believe that it could be

Beautiful, but deadly, rose?

Each and every rose I've treated

With most tender, loving care.

They do respond with pretty blooms;

If they're grateful, not aware.

Perils in my jungle garden

Include earwigs, snails, and slugs;

And, there could be, from time to time,

Nasty biting flies and bugs.

Tiger lilies, in golden glory,

Present tall and graceful view,

But they return my care for them

By making hair orangey hue.

Among tomatoes, cherry type

Reach for kitchen window top.

Those sweet one million grow and grow;

Wonder if they'll ever stop.

As for grapes, they grow on and on

Covering fence and many shrubs

With early promise of much fruit

To fill half a dozen tubs.

Persimmons sprawl and twist away

Over every rose and lily,

While kiwis, with their luscious fruit,

Produce vines willy-nilly.

Could carry on and tell you more,

But there really is no use.

Now, must go to tend my plants

Yes, and suffer more abuse.

De-Bugging

Bugging is illegal,

Starting in July.

False hopes all it raises;

There's good reason why.

The anti-bugging law

Bound to be a flop;

Bugging is a nuisance

Difficult to stop.

Here's one law can't enforce;

It won't last a day;

At least, in my garden,

Bugs won't go away.

Cute Robber

Day had been a busy one;

Planned an early night.

Glanced out to check the weather;

Beheld furry sight.

A robber racoon boldly

Walked atop the fence,

Heading for the tasty grapes;

Free meal made good sense.

We hurried out in the gloom

To chase thief away.

Bold racoon was not afraid.

On fence it did stay.

With sticks and shouts we were joined

By neighbours next door.

Soon discovered that there were

Pesky racoons four

They leaped from fence to roof top,

Blinking in disdain.

Left deposit in the eaves;

Jumped to fence again.

Don't care for masked marauders,

Though some call them cute.

But there will be all-out war

If they touch my fruit.

Our neighbours finally turned the trick

With a rock or two,

And racoons, all four, rambled off

With no fond adieu.

Those racoons may well steal from me;

Something else I lack.

You surely know you stole my heart;

I don't want it back.

Even Adam and Eve

Would you believe, all puns began

In Eden Garden, long ago,

When Adam was cast out, with Eve,

To plant, and weed, and hoe, hoe, hoe?

Told not to eat from certain tree,

Though, in days of unsprayed fruit,

For goodness snakes, what was to lose?

Not even Adam's unfrayed suit.

We know the rest, two nature buffs,

For bitten apple, welfare lost,

For what was Eden is no more;

Garden pear nipped by knowledge frost.

Shame keeper of the applesauce,

Poor Adam sighed, as well he might

When evil Sir bent Eden's law;

Sad moment Eve gave A-dam bite.

Autumn

Vapour-thin autumn air

Cuts with breath that slashes,

While wan and watery sun

Gently stirs warm ashes.

Weak summer's embers glow;

Brief warmth soon brushed away,

Fall's cool hand slowly shuts

Summer's door, day by day.

Sparks left from August's fire

Try autumn's might to flout,

Then finally subside;

Grey-brown mist swirls about.

Red-eyed sun squints in smog

As summer party ends

To leave dew-wet remains,

Tattered blooms, dead leaf blends.

Cool misty cloudy tide creeps up,

Yet blue awhile holds fast

And gains a bit by day;

But murky die is cast.

Last feeble flicker dies

As brimming pitcher spills'

Beneath grey, sodden lid

Covering all, sea to hills.

Garden Puzzle

To garden is one hobby

Of a few I pursue.

Of minuses and pluses

There have been quite a few.

The gains outweigh the losses;

But, if you would succeed

In the world of gardening,

Great patience you will need

One great mystery does exist,

Which puzzles me, alas;

It's all about garden's lawn,

And growing of the grass.

Not even experts can explain

Why lawn grass may fade,

But in flower beds persists'

And ever does invade.

Brief Beauty

When nature flaunts its colours,

As the summer fades away;

Gold and red, and in between;

Lighten up autumnal day.

Maples, with their scarlet flags,

Display brightly gaudy show,

While so many shrubs and trees

Banners wave with golden glow.

The coast mountains back-drop form;

Many shades of ever-green

Make a perfect palette for

Bright beauty of autumn scene.

Some leaves merely shrivel up

And fly before each gust.

As for stately horse-chestnut,

Leaves don't colour, they just rust.

All too soon it is over.

Cruel, chilly winds strip the trees

To skeletons, bare and gaunt,

Shaking naked in the breeze.

Spaced Out/Room Reserved

With fuchsias safely underground;

Some other plants need greenhouse care;

Cactus, ginger, tibouchina;

With banana already there.

Geraniums and all the rest

That cannot stand the winter's chill

Are placed on the shelves and the floor

As the greenhouse they all fill.

One thing is indeed, a worry.

With all those plants from roof to floor;

How can person take care of them?

Can't even get inside the door.

Treasure Trove

Climbed to far off pasture,

High up on rugged hill;

Gazed back at my home field;

Found it was greener still.

Fought way through thorny bush

To seek out berries sweet;

Returned to edge of patch;

Taste there could not be beat.

Yet, wonder if, somewhere

Around next bend could be

Something extra special;

Will have to wait and see.

Instead of searching for

Diamond-studded rainbow,

Dig around my own home ground;

Great treasures there will show.

Dangerous Fruit

Plant of vigour blackberry is;

Survives where others fail.

Produces fruit for those who dare,

As the thorns do impale.

Berries are so sweet and juicy

In blackberry patches,

With the trouble and with the pain

Of the stabs and scratches.

For jelly, jam and pie they're great;

Or to eat as you pick.

So why not enjoy this hard-earned treat,

As all your wounds you lick.

When you begin blackberry search,

To dye you must prepare,

As purple stain spreads over you,

And everything you wear.

As sure as sharp blackberry thorns,

There is something else that sticks;

The fact that we still care for us,

Despite the cruel fate tricks.

No matter if blackberries scratch,

And perhaps draw blood too,

It will not change the loving fact

That I am stuck on you.

Berry Challenge

Blackberry plant, invasion;

Never waits for invitation,

Give it an inch, and you will find.

Soon there'll be hopeless situation.

There is sweet, redeeming feature:

Bonus of delicious berry,

Which can produce tasty jelly;

But, with jam, of seeds be wary.

Picking berries can be challenge,

As one who knows the way to harvest;

And long time picker, can advise;

Bullet-proof clothing would suggest.

Machete can be quite useful,

But, no matter what care you take,

When picking is complete, you'll find

Sharp thorns that stab will misery make.

Though end result will be the same,

Experience may help a bit.

Have always had to pay the price;

And can show the wounds to prove it.

Blackberry Prize

Home-made blackberry jelly
Can be a gourmet delight:
But, as any picker knows,
First must win thorny fight.

Preparing for the struggle,
We both dressed with extra care;
With arms and legs well covered --
Only hands and face were bare.

We fought our way through brambles.
Ignoring each scratch and nick,
So that others could enjoy
Ebony fruit we did pick.

Finally, with brimming pails,
First stage of our task was done.
This was only beginning;
Soon final act had begun.

Hazel, with her kitchen skills,
Knew exactly what to do.
Our reward for this will be
Pleasure it will give to you.

No Roses But - -

It looks as if there'll be

No more roses for awhile;

Till they bloom once again,

Will you settle for a smile?

Tried hard to keep the blooms

Breaking forth for you each week,

But winter chill has made

Branches of each rose bush bleak.

A few violas fan

Waning spark of summer's flame;

Though they are so dainty,

Could never be quite the same.

Of course you could dust off

Artificial ones I sent,

But after all this time

Chances are they're slightly bent.

Here's a bit of green for you,

Your own personal holly tree;

If it should need attention,

Night or day, just call on me.

Mixed Match

Male or female holly,

Not easy to decide

Until crimson berries

Show which is blushing bride.

The tiny tree you have

Could be of either sex;

A nuisance not to know,

But does it really vex?

If holly needs a mate,

Can make a choice from five;

But time alone will tell

If matching pair survive

(to Jacquie)

Autumn Promise

The naked branches in the copse
Shake bleakly in the breeze,
As morning mists sun sweeps away,
Exposing gaunt, thin trees.

Mix of gold and crimson leaves
Remind of summer past,
When nature donned a cloak of green:
No thought of wintry blast.

Background mountains don winter caps,
But not to hibernate.
To skiers, and all who would slide,
There is a frosty date.

No matter how it blows and storms,
We know, for sure, one thing:
From the chilling cold of winter,

Forward we'll move, to Spring.

Winter Optimists

Perfect beets and peas and beans abound,

Though winter's frost still locks the ground;

And fruit canes shake to icy breath,

As Nature sleeps and seems near death.

Red, ripe tomatoes load each plant,

The bustling bees add busy chant;

Huge carrots toss their plumes, and yet,

Earth sleeps on, rigid, stiff and set..

Cobs of corn, so sweet and ;yellow;

Giant cabbage, firm and mellow,

Set off by flowers' countless hues;

But still, cold reigns with frigid views.

No magic this, for those who know;

First summer comes 'mid ice and snow.

As fancy dons the clothes of deeds,

Through pages in our book of seeds.

Plant-ation

Plant Plaint

Be sure to treat us with

The kindest T.L.C.

So we may continue

To be a sight to see.

Water when we need it

We will appreciate;

Don't let us get too dry;

But, then, don't inundate.

Keep us moist and happy;

Your kindness we'll repay'

We'll do our blooming best

To brighten up your day.

Plant Tune-Up

For those who sing and talk to plants

Here is the latest word;

Cucumbers love to hear the flute;

In case you hadn't heard.

There's faster sprouting beans and corn

When high-pitched notes assail.

Sing in falsetto when you plant;

Your crops will never fail.

If you should find plants don't respond,

There's no point in grumbling;

Just try a flute with higher pitch;

Shriek instead of mumbling.

(inspired by a CP wireservice story about

a University of Ottawa biology professor)

Plant Care

Have heard that T.L.C.

Will help a plant, indeed;

'Tis said that plants respond

To anger, love, and greed.

Could those who have green thumb

Know language of the plants?

Know how to soothe with songs,

Get extra growth with chants?

Can't believe plants tremble,

And sense destructive thoughts;

Unless, perhaps, the ones

That spend their lives in pots.

Have reached the conclusion

It's other way around;

Plants do frighten people,

And theory has sound ground.

Often, in the garden,

Have felt a pang of fear;

Uprooting dandelion,

Have heard a dozen sneer.

Your sympathy don't waste;

It's something plants don't need;

What is someone's flower

Is other person's weed.

Will be most carefull till

More facts they do amass;

Not hurt a living thing,

Nor cut a blade of grass.

Plant Life

House plants are getting restless;

Lie-detector probes their thoughts.

It's enough to curl their roots;

They're all shaking in their pots.

They have no society

To protect them in the ground,

No shelter that can save them,

Whether they are parched or drowned.

So treat your plants quite gently,

And be sure no care they lack.

If you wish, may talk to them;

Hardly think they'll answer back.

If your plants become distressed,

No point in giving candy;

Talk to them in soothing voice.

And polygraph keep handy.

(inspired by an AP wireservice

story from Westland, Mich.)

Miracle Aloe Vera

Had small aloe vera

In single pot alone

Knew its healing powers,

Which, of course, are well known.

Day by day, aloe grew,

And with shoots did expand.

IT really did branch out

And grew to beat the band.

Let aloe go its way;

No coddle and no fuss

As it produced more plants;

At least a dozen, plus.

If aloe continues,

Could start big plantation.

Have of them just enough

To supply small nation,

Magic aloe vera,

For cuts and burns has cure;

So you should have a plant;

Fell better, to be sure.

Golden Touch

The hardy tiger lily

Is, indeed, a real delight

Its beauty in the garden

Is always most welcome sight.

Oh so lovely to look at,

But of one thing must beware;

Admire it at distance,

Yet always approach with care.

The friendly tiger lily

All viewers should be aware,

Approaching it too closely,

You'll be crowned with golden hair.

One day, tiger lily waved,

And hair took on yellow hue.

Decided that snap-shot would

Prove golden touch was true.

Clear enough the picture was,

But, something not shown there

As top of head was cut off,

And, of course, could see no hair.

Others' Rows

Dig In

Now they're renting gardens

For the green of thumb

Who live in apartments;

From four walls are numb.

New trend may be started,

Box dwellers needs;

Fresh vegetables to grow

Among noxious weeds.

Those who live in houses,

Garden chores could bore;

Here's their chance to rent out

Weeding, tending chore.

Could go one step farther

And rent out a lawn;

Renter could mow and trim,

Use from dusk to dawn.

If apartment tenants

Wanted flowers too,

They could rent flower beds

Until blooms were through.

Best plan of all would be,

Just to buy the seeds,

Rent them out to others;

Take back pay in feeds.

Attention All Plant Sitters

Take good care of all my plants

And treat them with T.L.C.

Please don't forget to water,

Yet, too wet should never be.

Should you ever talk to them

Never build your hopes too high;

Only answer you may get

Is sad air-conditioned sigh.

Even if a plant does speak,

It won't have that much to tell

As I never speak to plant,

Unless it gives out a yell.

If all my plants fade and droop

Though for care they do not lack,

Don't worry as they'll perk up,

On the day that I get back.

Pot growth

To men who must smoke pot,

Here's something to beware;

Lest you find, on your chest'

You've grown much more than hair.

Some ladies might not mind,

If they want more, not less;

But, long-haired man or maid,

Most difficult to guess.

These days of equal rights,

Why shouldn't men smoke pot,

Even though they may grow

To fill bras wives have bought.

(Inspired by an AP item from Boston

in The Vancouver Sun newspaper)

Writings from Mythbreaker:

Archway series:

Archway: Six Year Book of Dreams (Vol. I)
Archway: Six Year Book of Dreams (Vol. II)
Archway: Lifetime Rhyme (Vol. I)
Archway: Lifetime Rhyme (Vol. II)
Archway's Christmas New Years Rhymes
Archway's Valentine Love
Archway's Garden Rhymes

Terrian Journals series:

A Sketch of Terrian History
Terrian Journals: Living as a Newcomer
Middle Earth Journals
Rediscovery Journals
Fukurokuju No Kasumi Journals
Sabbatical Journals
Departure Journals
Terrian Journals for the Misguided
Terrian Journals' N.S.R.: Not Spying, …Really!
TJ JNG: Terrian Journals' Jokes Nobody Gets
Terrian Journals First Anthology
Terrian Journals Second Anthology
Terrian Journals (periodical)

www.ingramcontent.com/pod-product-compliance
Lightning Source LLC
Chambersburg PA
CBHW042335150426
43194CB00005B/164